The Year of
Hope and Fear

The Year of Hope and Fear

Insurrection & Repression, 1919

Eric Leif Davin

DavinBooks
P.O. Box 90087
Pittsburgh, PA 15224

The Year of Hope and Fear
Insurrection & Repression, 1919

ISBN 978-1-716-02359-0

An earlier version of this essay was presented at the Homestead (PA) Pumphouse in April, 2019, at the Battle of Homestead Foundation's Commemoration of the 100th Anniversary of the Great Steel Strike of 1919 and was published in the 2019 issue of the *Pennsylvania Labor History Journal*.

Front Cover:
Kirby in the New York *World*, October 11, 1919

The Great Steel Strike

The horrors of the Great War, as World War I was then known, ended in Europe on November 11, 1918. Over the course of the next year, 1919, the hope of utopia, and the fear of a new tyranny, followed as the continent was engulfed in insurrection and reaction.

In America, 1919 also brought hope and fear, the hope of a new era of working class empowerment, and the fear that such working class empowerment threatened the basic fabric of American society.

Central to those American hopes, as well as fears, was the great steel strike of 1919. It was the largest single strike in American history up to that time. At its height over a third of a million steelworkers, mostly of immigrant background, were on strike. For them, it promised to bring about the long-sought unionization of the core industry of America's industrial economy. For those who opposed them, the strike threatened both the very nature of the American economic model, as well as America itself.

Understanding the hopes of the workers, and the fears of those who fought them, also helps us understand why the strike was such a titanic confrontation. For both sides it was a battle for the soul of America, a battle for what it meant to be an "American." That battle, however, was fought in the context of even larger struggles that same bloody year.

Revolution in Europe

The end of the Great War brought about the destruction of four great and powerful empires. These were the Romanov, the Hohenzollern, and the Hapsburg in Europe and, in the Middle East, the Ottoman Empire. In the wake of their destruction, a wave of utopian ferment swept across Europe, and a just-ended war that many viewed as an imperialist war segued into an international class war that seemed, somehow, connected to events in Russia.

The first empire to collapse, even before the war ended, was the Romanov in Russia. What replaced it by the end of 1917 was a revolutionary, class-conscious, and militant Bolshevik communist government beset on all sides by forces that threatened to destroy it. Throughout the crucial year of 1919 this government battled military intervention from the Allied powers of France, Britain, Greece, and America, all attempting to overthrow it.

At the same time, the Bolsheviks were fighting a vicious civil war against counter-revolutionary armies in central and eastern Siberia; in Ukraine, where another such army threatened to take Moscow; and in the north, where yet another such army came within miles of capturing Petrograd, the original heart of the

Bolshevik Revolution.

The next empire to fall was that of the Hohenzollern in Germany. It, too, collapsed before the war ended. Indeed, its very collapse ended the war. The German homefront had been rife with grumblings of discontent for years. Industrial strikes and hunger demonstrations had threatened the war effort since 1916.

At the beginning of November, 1918, the last month of the war, the German Grand Fleet at Kiel was ordered to sally out to engage in a suicidal battle with the British Grand Fleet. Instead, the 30,000 sailors of the fleet mutinied. They formed a sailors' soviet modeled after those in Russia and demanded the abdication of the Kaiser, an end to martial law, and the liberation of all military and political prisoners.

In its wake, mutiny and rebellion quickly swept all across Germany. In Hamburg, mutinous sailors stormed the army barracks and then led a crowd of angry workers in smashing their way into the city hall, where they demanded the resignation of the city council. In Frankfurt, crowds attacked army officers and deposed the Chief of Police, replacing him with a professor from the local university.

On November 7th, in Munich, the largest city in Bavaria, a socialist journalist named Kurt Eisner proclaimed a socialist revolution and led a crowd of workers into the local army barracks and seized arms and ammunition. The soldiers joined them in their revolt.

Germany had only been formed out of myriad principalities and small kingdoms at the end of the Franco-Prussian War in 1870, and many of these entities retained an ambiguous quasi-independence. Such was the case in Bavaria. The evening of November 7th, King Ludwig III of Bavaria and his family fled Munich, and the insurgents proclaimed the independent Bavarian Soviet Republic, with Eisner at its head.

On November 8th, sailors invaded the castle of the Duke of Brunswick and also demanded his abdication. He did so, declaring that he put the local government "into the hands of the Soldiers' and Workers' Council." Similar actions happened elsewhere across Germany that same day.

On November 9th the Kaiser himself abdicated, and fled with his family to Holland. A caretaker government in Berlin, led by the Social Democratic Party (SPD), took over, but the situation in Berlin remained chaotic. Karl Liebknecht, a leader of the more radical Spartacus League, led a crowd of armed workers in seizing the Imperial Palace and proclaiming a German Soviet Republic. At the same time, the socialists of the SPD proclaimed a liberal German Republic at the Reichstag.

The next day, November 10th, the Berlin Workers' and Soldiers' Councils chose a six man council, dominated by the SPD, as the first government of the new German Republic. And, on the day after that, November 11th, the Great War ended.

Meanwhile, the Austro-Hungarian Empire dissolved and the ruling and long-lived House of Hapsburg ceased to exist. That empire splintered into a balkanized collection of successor states. The Austrian Social Democrats took over in Vienna and a Soviet Republic, seeking an alliance with the Russian Bolsheviks, took power in Hungary.

Counter-Revolution

By the end of 1918 revolution was on the march everywhere across central Europe, as were minor civil wars. But, "Civil war," declared Rosa Luxemburg, the co-leader with Karl Liebknecht of the Spartacists, "is only another name for class war." At a two-day Spartacus conference in Berlin that began on December 29th, the Spartacists changed their name to the German Communist Party.

Meanwhile, conditions became even more volatile in Berlin. At the end of December, a radicalized military unit of the Imperial Army rebelled and seized the Imperial Palace and the Chancellery. The new Spartacist-Communist Party joined the revolt, and occupied the police headquarters and the office of the Social Democratic newspaper.

The Social Democratic government fled Berlin and moved many of its administrative functions to the city of Weimar. From there it called upon the Imperial Army to retake Berlin. The army obeyed only half-heartedly. In truth, the Imperial Army had almost completely dissolved with the end of the war, and could hardly be said to exist, as most of its rank and file deserted and simply went home. The Social Democratic government therefore called upon the myriad Freikorps units to suppress the Spartacist uprising.

The Freikorps were para-military militias of well-armed, well-disciplined, embittered veterans of the former Imperial Army who refused to just go home after the Armistice. There were more than 150 such *ad hoc* groups of such veterans spread across Germany, commanded by such ex-officers of the Imperial Army as Captain Erwin Rommel, the future hero of North Africa. They painted swastikas on their helmets, paraded and trained in military uniforms, and refused to concede that Germany had militarily lost the war. Rather, according to the Big Lie they all proclaimed, Germany had been "stabbed in the back" by domestic traitors, such as the Spartacists. The Nazi Storm Troopers, into which these Freikorps militias would eventually be merged, were just one of such militias. All, however, were eager to answer the socialist government's call to suppress the communist uprisings in Berlin, Munich, and elsewhere.

The Freikorps reconquest of Berlin began on January 4th, 1919, and fighting continued until January 10th. Over 100 Spartacist rebels died in the fighting, with another 400 wounded. So ended the communist revolution in Berlin.

On January 15th, Freikorps paramilitaries burst into the clandestine safe house where Karl Liebknecht and Rosa Luxemburg were hiding. Both were taken to Freikorps headquarters, where they were beaten and then shot. Luxemburg's body was dumped into a canal, where it was not found until March, badly decomposed.

The Spartacist leaders were dead, but Spartacism, the spirit of revolt, was not. There were subsequent riots, strikes, and large demonstrations in Bremen, Hamburg, Dusseldorf, Essen, and Wilhelmshaven. Meanwhile, the Bavarian Soviet Republic still remained to be dealt with.

On February 21st, a dispossessed nobleman assassinated Kurt Eisner, the head of the Bavarian Soviet Republic. His government, however, survived and became even more radical in the wake of his death.

On May 1st, the Freikorps fought their way into Munich and seized control of the city after three days of savage fighting. Over 700 defenders were killed in the battle, and thousands arrested. The leaders of the Soviet Republic were shot or sentenced to long prison terms.

The Hungarian Soviet Republic lasted a while longer. By August 1st, however, the newly formed Romanian Army fought its way into Budapest and overthrew the revolutionary government. The Romanian Army instituted a reign of terror in Budapest in which thousands were shot, thousands jailed, and thousands sent to forced labor camps. When it left the city in mid-November it left behind a military dictatorship in Hungary that continued the anti-Leftist terror.

Mutiny Among the Allies

The spirit of revolt, however, was alive even within the armies of the Allied powers. At the end of January, at the same time the Freikorps consolidated its conquest of Berlin, British troops in the French port of Calais mutinied and held the city for four days.

The spirit of revolt was even stronger among the French forces intervening in Ukraine against the Bolsheviks. On January 30th, French infantry and artillery units refused to join in an attack on the Red Army in Bessarabia (now called Moldova). On March 7th, other French units refused to reinforce allied Greek forces in Kherson, allowing the Red Army to capture that town.

Early in April French units in Odessa refused to defend the city against a Red Army attack. Greek soldiers were ordered to surround and disarm the mutinous French troops, but refused to do so. On April 5th, Odessa had to be evacuated. Allied troops marched out of Odessa lustily singing the revolutionary anthem, *The Internationale*.

Then the French Black Sea fleet mutinied. On April 16th, sailors in the fleet off Sevastopol in the Crimea refused to bombard the Red Army then besieging the city. Sailors, also singing *The Internationale*, imprisoned their officers and hoisted red flags. A delegation of sailors presented the admiral commanding the fleet with their ultimatums:

1) An end to the military intervention in Russia and an immediate return to France; and

2) Rapid demobilization.

Otherwise, they vowed, they would hand the French fleet over to the Bolsheviks.

French soldiers deserting the fortress in the city joined a march of sailors to the Sevastopol Town Hall, where they declared their support to the Chairman of the Revolutionary Committee. When Allied Greek soldiers began firing on the French soldiers and sailors, French gunners back on the French fleet began to shell the Greek battleship in the harbor until the Greeks ceased firing.

Rebellion at Home

Events at home were just as disturbing to the authorities. The Swiss Army suppressed a general strike in all major Swiss cities. In February the Catalonian anarcho-syndicalist Confederation of Labor (CNT) led 100,000 workers out in a one-month general strike in the Barcelona region of Spain. The unrest then spread south to large general strikes in Seville and Granada, and a wave of anarchist insurgency erupted among the peasants of Andalusia.

On January 25th, 26 labor unions in Belfast, Ireland, launched a one-month general strike. The British government, a colonial power that still ruled Ireland, imposed martial law and sent the strike leaders to prison.

The next day, January 26th, the Glasgow Trades Council in Scotland called a general strike in that city. Glasgow was the center of the syndicalist movement in Great Britain and the government quickly moved to suppress the strike by imposing martial law. As in Belfast, the strike leaders were sent to prison.

But when 600,000 British railroad workers later struck in protest against a rollback of wages to a level even lower than before the war, the government was unsure if the British army was loyal enough to be used against them. It ended the strike by agreeing that wages would be kept at the war level.

All of these events were given panic coverage in American newspapers. To them it seemed that Bolshevism was on the march everywhere. Their panic was heightened by a wave of domestic strikes throughout the year 1919. Over the course of 1919 over 3,600 strikes in America brought out over four million workers, 20% of the American workforce. Further, the number of strikes increased as the year went on. And, as the strike wave grew, so did the hysteria of the authorities and their fear of Bolshevism in America.

The New Unionism in America

Indeed, the Russian Revolution, and subsequent post-war events in Europe, did inspire American industrial workers, who were mostly of immigrant background, and who came from those very regions of southern and eastern Europe now in revolutionary turmoil following the departure of the kings.

Despite the fears of the American authorities, however, this was not because these immigrant industrial workers necessarily shared the ideology of the Russian and other Marxist revolutionaries. Rather, it was because there were revolutions in their homelands at all. For centuries, wealthy nobles and tyrannical czars of various kinds had ruled the ancestral homelands of vast numbers of America's immigrant industrial workers. Change had seemed to be impossible.

Now, back home, the czar had been deposed, the Kaiser had fled, and the old nobility had been overthrown. If that could happen in their old homelands, it inspired in them the hope that tyrannical corporate czars could also be overthrown in their new homeland, in America.

However, this would not be done through armed insurrection. It would be done through their unions, and the concept of a "New Unionism" which many of those unions espoused.

The concept of the New Unionism was not a precise ideology. Rather, it was a general term for the new style of union organizing that was taking root at the time. It included the belief in increased militancy, of fighting back against the adverse conditions brought on by the Second Industrial Revolution that had reshaped the American economy since the 1890s.

It also preached the idea of "industrial unionism," of industry-wide unionization, in opposition to the old separate craft unionism espoused by the American Federation of Labor (AFL). There was, for example, no one steelworkers union in steel, the largest manufacturing sector of the American economy. Instead, there were myriad unions covering workers in various jobs within the steel mills. The concept of industrial unionism meant that all workers in a certain industry would be organized into one big union, regardless of their specific jobs. This was for practical reasons. Simply put, you had to have a big army to fight a big army, and the old specialized and separate craft unions made it easy for the giant and monolithic corporations to divide and conquer the workers.

But the new industrial unions and organizations espousing New Unionism not only viewed themselves as "fighting unions," they also viewed themselves as "educational unions." They also preached industrial unionism for ideological reasons. They argued that all workers, perhaps all workers in the world, should, eventually, belong to “One Big Union.” Once this happened, then real change would come.

And that real change was the long-term vision of the New Unionism. Thus, they tied mundane union activities to the long-term goal of either extensive radical reform, as in the case of most of such unions, or of anti-capitalist revolution (as in the case of the Industrial Workers of the World, the IWW).

These new unions, therefore, saw themselves as more than just workplace bargaining agents, seeking only higher wages and better working conditions, as did the “pure and simple” craft unions of the AFL. They also saw themselves as educational and political organizations working to change society as a whole. They saw themselves as the hope for a better world for all.

And, at the same time that the events in Russia and Europe sent shivers of fear down the spines of the authorities, it gave hope to those espousing the New Unionism in America that a new and better age was dawning.

The American Strike Wave

And so militant strikes proclaiming the ideas of the New Unionism proliferated in 1919, spreading both hope and fear across the land. The first major one of these was in Lawrence, Massachusetts. Lawrence was the scene of a dramatic IWW-led textile strike in 1912, the "Bread and Roses" strike, that ended in victory for the workers and spread the fame of the IWW as a fighting union. In 1919, however, the Lawrence textile workers still worked nine-hour days, still worked six days a week, and they still wanted an eight-hour day, with no reduction in pay.

On February 3rd they launched a strike of all textile workers in Lawrence and, once more, called upon the IWW for help. The federal government had almost crippled the IWW the previous summer with a mass trial that had sentenced IWW-leader Big Bill Haywood and 100 other top IWW leaders to long prison terms for opposition to the Great War. In February another 54 foreign-born IWWs were deported.

However, Carlo Tresca and Arturo Giovannitti, two leaders of the successful 1912 strike, had avoided both prison and deportation. These famous, and radical, strike leaders returned to Lawrence in 1919 to again help lead the strike, which then dragged on for months.

On February 6th, three days after the Lawrence textile strike began, a general strike erupted in Seattle. Earlier, well over 35,000 shipyard workers in that West Coast city had walked out demanding higher wages and shorter hours. Now, the Seattle Central Labor Council, representing all unions in that West Coast city, called out every worker in Seattle to support them. The Central Labor Council felt it had to respond in that fashion in order to "promote labor solidarity against the growing militancy of employers." Sixty thousand Seattle workers, representing almost every trade in the city and imbued with the idea of labor solidarity, answered the call.

The local newspapers were already filled with denunciations of the on-going "Bolshevik revolutions" in Belfast and Glasgow and they hysterically linked the Seattle general strike to events overseas. "This is America, not Russia," cried *The Star*. The *Post-Intelligencer* ran a front-page cartoon showing a red flag flying above the Stars and Stripes. Headlines in other newspapers across the country cried, "Reds Directing Seattle Strike – To Test Chance for Revolution." In Seattle, declared the Cleveland *Plain Dealer*, "the Bolshevik beast had come into the open." It was "only a middling step from Petrograd to Seattle," warned the *Chicago Tribune*.

Seattle Mayor Ole Hanson declared that the general strike was part of an IWW plot to launch a "revolutionary holocaust" in America.

The strikers, who comprised virtually every worker in Seattle, were – every one of them, he said – all red revolutionaries who "want to take possession of our American Government and try to duplicate the anarchy of Russia." He called for U.S. Army troops from a nearby military base to take control of the city and impose martial law.

On February 6th, in a car draped in the Stars and Stripes, Mayor Hanson led the U. S. Army into Seattle. He called upon the Central Labor Council to end the general strike, or see it crushed in blood by military force. On February 10th, the Council called off the strike. "The rebellion is quelled," proudly proclaimed Mayor Hanson. *The Star* agreed, saying, "Today this Bolshevik-sired nightmare is at an end." The *Post-Intelligencer* declared, "From Russia they came, and to Russia they should be made to go!"

A few weeks later, Canadian labor radicals just across the border in Calgary launched a new nation-wide labor organization to be explicitly known as the "One Big Union." Declaring that global class war was a reality, they referred to the Central Committee of the projected One Big Union as the "Central Soviet." Provincial committees were to be known as "Provincial Soviets." As if to confirm this global class war, the next month, in March, Russian Bolsheviks formed the Third International (the "Comintern") of all existing and potential global communist parties, headquartered in Moscow.

The Red Scare

Perhaps in response to all this, U.S. Secretary of Labor William B. Wilson warned that, "The recent strikes in Lawrence, Seattle, and other places were not industrial, economic disputes in their origin, but were results of a deliberate, organized attempt at a social and political movement to establish Soviet Governments in the United States."

U. S. Secretary of War Newton Baker agreed, saying, "Since the Armistice, there has been a growing agitation and unrest evidenced by wide-spread industrial controversies. Our newspapers are filled with accounts of violent agitation by so-called Bolsheviks and radicals courting violence and urging action in behalf of what they call revolution."

These Cabinet secretaries were part of a rising chorus of voices in the spring of 1919 warning of the Red menace to America. Not least among these voices were those of the judges on the U. S. Supreme Court. In March, 1919, the Supreme Court handed down three unanimous decisions that went far in gutting American civil liberties.

In the first of these, *Schenck v. United States,* the court unanimously upheld a lower court conviction of a defendant who had mailed pamphlets during the war urging potential army inductees to resist the draft. Writing for the unanimous court, Justice Oliver Wendell Holmes, Jr., declared that, "when a nation is at war many things that might be said in time of peace are such a hindrance to its effort that their utterance will not be endured."

He then articulated his famous "clear and present danger" doctrine. "The question," he declared, "is whether the words are used in such circumstances and are of such a nature to create a clear and present danger that they will bring about the substantive evils that Congress has a right to prevent."

Holmes' "clear and present danger" test greatly reduced the scope of protected freedom of speech in the United States. However, Holmes and the court went even further in the second case that month, *Frohwerk v. United States*. In this case the court again unanimously upheld the conviction of the defendant for simply writing an article in which he questioned the purpose of the European war, and also questioned the constitutionality of the military draft.

In the third case, *Debs v. the United States,* the court unanimously upheld the conviction of Eugene V. Debs, leader of the Socialist Party. Debs had delivered his standard speech attacking capitalism and questioning the economic causes of the war at a Socialist Party convention in Canton, Ohio. Debs had not spoken to potential draftees, nor had he explicitly urged violation of draft laws. Even so, the court upheld his conviction, with Holmes declaring that, "if a part of the manifest intent of the more general utterances was to encourage those present to obstruct the recruiting service," it was not constitutionally protected free speech. Debs, therefore, was to be sent off to serve long years in federal prison.

These Supreme Court decisions in March went far in enacting previously unknown restrictions on free speech, and in endorsing the on-going all-out assault on radical or dissenting opinions then raging all across America.

In response, in April Congress barred Socialist Party leader Victor Berger of Milwaukee from taking the seat in the U. S. House of Representatives to which he had been elected the previous November. A special election was called to fill his now vacant seat.

But none of this quelled the strike wave roiling the nation. On April 15th, all of New England was plunged into silence as 20,000 telephone operators, led by the Boston local of the Telephone Workers' Union, struck. However, as in strikes elsewhere, the mostly female workforce was not interested in revolution. They earned only $16 a week, and they wanted $22 a week. After a week without telephone service in the region, they were offered $19 a week. They accepted, and phone service was restored. The New England telephone strike disrupted and alarmed the business community, and seemed to be yet one more ominous sign of the times.

A more dangerous omen was the series of "May Day" bombs mailed to numerous prominent men at the end of the month. On April 28th, a bomb was detected before it exploded in the mail of Seattle Mayor Ole Hanson. Another bomb sent to Georgia's ex-Senator Thomas Hardwick blew off both hands of his black maid as she opened it.

Alerted to the danger, on April 30th the vigilant U. S. Postal Service discovered another 34 bombs mailed to:

*Secretary of Labor William B. Wilson;

*U. S. Attorney General A. Mitchell Palmer;

*Supreme Court Justice Oliver Wendell Holmes, Jr. (who, on March 10th had delivered the unanimous Supreme Court decision upholding the prison sentence of Eugene V. Debs for violating the war-time Espionage Act);

*The Chairman of the U. S. Senate Bolshevik Investigating Committee;

*Postmaster General Albert Burleson (who had banned radical literature from the mails);

*Judge Kenesaw Mountain Landis (who had presided over the big IWW trial during the war that destroyed the IWW, and who had sentenced Big Bill Haywood and the other top IWW leaders to prison);

*Frederick C. Howe (Ellis Island's Commissioner of Immigration);

*and both John D. Rockefeller and J. P.

Morgan.

Newspapers across the land screamed, "Reds Plan May Day Murders." Criminal anarchy laws blossomed across the land in the resulting national hysteria.

Until 1919, May Day had never taken on the political significance in America that it had developed in Europe. But in 1919 radicals across the country planned big parades to celebrate the Russian Revolution. Major disturbances took place on May 1st in New York City, Cleveland, and Boston, as ex-soldiers battled Leftist militants.

Later that month, the American Legion, a patriotic veterans' organization, was founded as America's pale version of Germany's Freikorps. Its new commandant, Colonel Franklin d'Olier of Philadelphia, declared, "The Legion will combat Bolshevism and incendiary radicalism all the way." By the end of the year the Legion boasted one million ex-soldiers as members, all ready to do battle with the Reds. They greatly outnumbered the IWW, which, despite the repression it suffered, still struggled on. At its annual convention that same month, it claimed only 33,000 members.

Two weeks after the May Day battles, on May 15th, the Winnipeg general strike erupted in Canada. Its origin was a strike by the city's metal trades unions demanding, not revolution, but shorter hours and higher wages. In solidarity, the Winnipeg Trades and Labour Council called for a general strike.

Despite its purely economic origin, the authorities saw it as yet another Bolshevik uprising. Newspapers in the United States gave it the full Red Scare treatment, reporting many horror stories, none of which were true. A "Citizens' Committee" in the city organized a middle-class para-military force to patrol the city, as the 30,000 strikers in Winnipeg also comprised the police and other municipal workers. On June 17th, this civilian vigilante group arrested the strike leaders. On June 21st the Royal Canadian Mounted Police took control of the city and, on June 25th, after six weeks of turmoil, the Winnipeg Trades and Labour Council called off the general strike.

Meanwhile, on June 2nd, yet another general strike erupted, this time in Vancouver, in solidarity with the Winnipeg general strike. The Vancouver general strike lasted until early July.

At the same time that the Winnipeg and Vancouver general strikes continued, a second wave of bombs exploded in eight American cities on the night of June 2nd. One bomb damaged the home of a Boston judge. Another damaged the home of a Massachusetts State Representative who had sponsored an anti-anarchy bill in the state legislature. Another bomb demolished the porch and front of the home of a Pittsburgh Plate Glass Company official who lived at 5437 Aylesboro Avenue in the wealthy Pittsburgh neighborhood of Squirrel Hill. The next-door home of federal judge W. H. S. Thompson was also severely damaged in the explosion. In the Pittsburgh suburb of Sheraden another bomb targeted the home of W. W. Sibray, an immigration official who was active in the effort to deport western Pennsylvania immigrants suspected of radicalism.

The most prominent target that night was, yet again, Attorney General A. Mitchell Palmer. The powerful bomb at his Washington, D. C. home exploded just as he was going to bed. It blew off the front of his house, although he was not harmed. It also damaged the home of Assistant Secretary of the Navy Franklin D. Roosevelt, who lived just across the street, jolting him awake.

The bomb, however, had detonated prematurely, blowing its carrier to pieces. His head was found on a rooftop several blocks away. He was identified as Carlo Valdinoce, a New Jersey anarchist. A manifesto found near each of the explosions, from Pittsburgh to Washington, D. C., to Boston read, in part, "There will have to be bloodshed. We will destroy and rid the world of your tyrannical institutions. Long live the social revolution." It was signed, "The Anarchist Fighters."

In response, Attorney General Palmer declared war on the bombers. He proposed yet more stringent anti-radical laws. He also launched an all-out manhunt for the bombers, and all other subversives, to be organized by a special

Anti-Radical Division of the Department of Justice under the direction of a young J. Edgar Hoover. This Anti-Radical Division was the precursor to the Federal Bureau of Investigation (FBI), which Hoover went on to lead for decades thereafter.

In the midst of all this, the Socialist Party, with 100,000 official members, met at its annual convention in Chicago. Inspired by the Russian Revolution, 70,000 members split from the party to form two rival new communist parties. One, calling itself the Communist Labor Party and led by radical journalist John Reed, among others, represented the American-born element with about 10,000 members. The rest, representing the foreign language federations within the party, formed the American Communist Party. The national hysteria over the perceived Red menace increased, and *The Pittsburgh Post* urged the firing squad for all such radicals.

The Boston Police Strike

And still the number of strikes increased across the nation. In April there were 248 strikes. In June there were 303 strikes. In July there were 360 strikes. On July 4th, over 5,000 New England fishermen, followed by maritime workers, began a 38-day strike.

That same Fourth of July, the U. S. Army deployed for a feared nation-wide Red-led general strike. Newspapers across the country screamed in bold headlines that there were "Plans for Widespread Violence and Murder," in which "Stolen Explosives Were To Be Used" to establish "A Reign of Terror."

Two companies of the army's Fourteenth Infantry were sent to Chicago to supplement the city's police force, already on full alert and reinforced by 1,000 volunteer deputies. Thirty well-armed U. S. Army soldiers were stationed at the Federal Building in Boston. Philadelphia streets were "filled with policemen," as were the streets of San Francisco. Police across the Bay in Oakland arrested and jailed known radicals as an "insurance device." But, except for the strike by New England fishermen that coincidentally began that day, nothing happened. However, on July 13th, Boston transit workers struck, stopping all public transportation in the city.

Then a yet more worrisome menace

appeared. At its June convention in Atlantic City, the American Federation of Labor (AFL) declared that it was prepared to grant charters to police unions. By August, the police forces of 37 large cities had been accepted into the AFL.

The police in Boston also unanimously expressed interest in unionizing and joining the AFL. The police commissioner and the mayor of Boston adamantly opposed that possibility. After months of fruitless negotiations, the entire Boston police force therefore walked off the job on September 16th.

There was no alternative police force to take its place. Riots and looting broke out in downtown Boston, resulting in hundreds of thousands of dollars in lost or damaged property. Boston seemed to have become an American Petrograd. "Lenin and Trotsky Are On Their Way," warned the *Wall Street Journal* in a headline. "Bolshevism in the United States is no longer a specter," declared the *Philadelphia Public Ledger*. "Boston in chaos reveals its sinister substance."

In response, the little-known Republican Massachusetts Governor, Calvin Coolidge, telegrammed AFL chief Samuel Gompers saying, "There is no right to strike against the public safety by anybody, anywhere, at any time." He also permanently fired the entire Boston police force and sent in the state's National Guard to establish military rule in the city.

Order was restored to Boston, and an

entirely new police force was recruited. Soon thereafter Coolidge signed legislation, quickly passed by the state legislature, establishing the Massachusetts State Police.

Coolidge's tough response to the crisis resulted in his overwhelming re-election as governor in that November's election. The next year his new fame carried him into the Vice Presidency and, soon thereafter, into the White House as the 30th President of the United States.

The Great Steel Strike

It was in this atmosphere of hope and hysteria that 250,000 steelworkers, soon to be 350,000, launched their nation-wide strike. The Boston police strike was only two days old when the nation's press announced that a strike in the steel industry to gain the right to unionize would begin on September 22nd.

The steel industry was the linchpin of the American economy, upon which hundreds of other economic sectors depended. It was, however, completely un-unionized. It had been so ever since the Carnegie Steel Co. had crushed the old Amalgamated Association of Iron and Steel Workers in the infamous Homestead Lockout and Strike of 1892. Its mostly immigrant workforce worked long and brutal hours in hellish conditions for less pay than would support the average American family. Nor had the American Federation of Labor (AFL), with its craft union orientation, exhibited much interest in organizing this immigrant, industrial, workforce.

But the federal government, concerned to keep industrial production humming, had been supportive of organized labor during the war. Because of that, workers had won temporary wage hikes. These gains were soon lost, however, in post-war inflation. Even so, this support encouraged labor's hopes that circumstances had changed and that the steel industry could be unionized, something that had eluded them during the war.

Thus, in August, 1918, just three months before the end of the war, the leaders of thirty large unions met to form the National Committee for Organizing Iron and Steel Workers. Their efforts eventually led to the call for an industry-wide steel strike scheduled to begin in September of 1919.

The subsequent steel strike was the biggest single strike in American history up to that time, and was to last for over three months, into 1920. If possible, the strike drove the authorities into even more hysteria. The fact that William Z. Foster, a former IWW organizer, led the strike only added to the resulting anti-red, anti-labor hysteria.

Eight years earlier, when Foster was still in the IWW, he had authored a pamphlet entitled *Syndicalism*, which was now reprinted by the authorities and widely distributed. This no doubt garnered more readers for Foster's pamphlet than in its original publication. In it he declared, "The wage system must be abolished. The thieves at present in control must be stripped of their booty and industry so reorganized that every individual shall have free access to the means of production.... The syndicalist knows he is engaged in a life and death struggle.... With him the end justifies the means."

Such previous statements by Foster led

Ohio's U. S. Representative John G. Cooper to brand him as unfit for "the name of an American citizen and the protection of that flag." Senator Charles S. Thomas of Colorado called him a radical who only sought economic chaos. Senator Henry L. Myers, of Montana, called him "a notorious syndicalist, revolutionist, and enemy of organized government."

The fact that nearly 70% of the striking steelworkers were of immigrant southern and eastern European background made it easier to label the strikers as un-American "Hunkies" and suspect in their loyalty. "The foreign element," charged *The New York Times*, "is steeped in the doctrines of the class war."

President Woodrow Wilson also fanned the flames of anti-radical and anti-immigrant sentiment. "The poison of disorder," he declared, "the poison of revolt, the poison of chaos" had entered "into the veins of this free people.... Any man who carries a hyphen about with him carries a dagger that he is ready to plunge into the vitals of this Republic."

Thus, the corporations and public authorities unleashed unrestrained and fearful repression on the strikers, with the full support of mainstream public opinion. Armed guards surrounded steel mills and thousands of "special deputies" patrolled the mill towns. Robert K. Murray, in his book, *Red Scare: A Study in National Hysteria, 1919-1920*, said that, "It was estimated, for example, that along the

Monongahela River from Pittsburgh to Clairton (a distance of twenty miles), 25,000 men were under arms at the onset of the strike, and that in some areas there was a deputy sheriff for almost every striker."

Picket lines were brutally dispersed, strikers arrested and jailed and sometimes killed, and free speech became a crime. Club swinging state policemen rode their horses onto the sidewalks and even into saloons and other businesses and into the living rooms of company houses. In Farrell, Pennsylvania, the police killed four strikers on the picket line and badly wounded eleven others. "The net result of such police activity," stated Murray, "was that in many areas civil liberty became a dead letter."

In the steel town of Gary, Indiana, (named after Judge Elbert Gary, the CEO of U. S. Steel) the federal government sent in the U.S. Army, under the command of General Leonard Wood, to place the city under martial law. General Wood had commanded the Rough Riders in Cuba during the Spanish-American war, was the former Chief of Staff of the U.S. Army, and had been the Military Governor of Cuba. Now he became the military governor of Gary, completely locking down the city. He immediately ordered Army intelligence officers to begin investigating striking steel workers in order to ferret out alleged Reds. His harsh military rule in Gary made him a leading contender for the Republican presidential nomination the next year, and he actually led the balloting at the nominating convention on the first four roll calls.

Despite the deliberately stoked hysteria over supposed Bolshevik influence among the strikers, both sides knew at bottom that, as David Brody observed in his book, *Crisis in Steel*, the steel strike wasn't about Bolshevik revolution. Nor, said Brody, was it over wages, hours or conditions. "It was over unionism itself. Organized labor was demanding that it represent and bargain for the steelworkers. The industry could not surrender on that point without surrendering managerial prerogatives" Both sides, therefore, saw it as an existential struggle, with management routinely calling the closed union shop "sovietism in disguise." Indeed, they charged, labor unionism itself "is nothing less than Bolshevism."

Meanwhile, other battles were being fought. On November 1st, the United Mine Workers, under the leadership of acting president John L. Lewis, led 400,000 mine workers out in a strike demanding an industry-wide contract, a 60% wage increase, a six-hour day and a five-day week. John L. Lewis was a registered Republican, and, at that time, a bitter anti-communist. Nevertheless, coal operators charged that Lenin and Trotsky had directly ordered the strike, and that it was financed by Moscow gold. The strike lasted until December 10th, and was finally settled when the miners won a 14% wage hike, with the promise of arbitration on their other demands.

On November 7th, the second anniversary of the Bolshevik Revolution, U. S. Attorney General A. Mitchell Palmer began his "Palmer Raids" against suspected radicals. His agents raided labor and leftist organizations in 18 cities, arresting hundreds.

On November 11th, the first anniversary of the end of the Great War, local members of the newly formed American Legion led a patriotic parade in the small town of Centralia, Washington. Some time earlier they had invaded and wrecked the local hall of the IWW. The IWW local soon repaired the hall. Now American Legionnaires broke off from the parade to wreck the hall again.

Wesley Everest, a member of the IWW local and himself an Army veteran of the Great War, confronted them. He was wearing his Army uniform and held a rifle in his hands. He fired into the attacking mob, killing four. The Legionnaires captured him, beat him, castrated him, strangled him, and lynched him from a nearby bridge. Then they used his uniformed corpse for target practice. After his murder, a reign of terror against the IWW smashed that union in the Washington timber forests.

On November 15th Palmer's men raided and wrecked the IWW headquarters in New York City. In Kansas City 27 IWW members were sentenced to a total of 123 years in prison on charges of "conspiracy against the government."

In December Socialist leader Victor Berger was again denied his seat in the U. S. House of Representatives for a second time, after winning the special election to fill his vacant seat in Milwaukee.

On December 21st, 250 Russian so-called "radical" immigrants were packed onto a dilapidated transport ship, dubbed the "Red Ark," and deported to Russia without benefit of a trial. The vast majority of them were simply common workingmen who happened to belong to the Union of Russian Workers, and who were entirely ignorant of political ideology.

However, two of the passengers were the notorious anarchists Emma Goldman and Alexander Berkman. The latter had attempted to assassinate steel master Henry Clay Frick during the 1892 steel lockout and strike in Homestead, Pennsylvania. Neither would ever again set foot in the United States.

On January 2nd in the new year of 1920, more of Palmer's raids in 23 cities seized 4,000 suspected radicals. In Boston 800 of them were marched in chains to the dockside for shipping to prison on Deer Island in Boston Harbor. In Detroit another 800 were held incommunicado in a derelict public building and denied the right to counsel. In Lynn, Massachusetts, 39 men were arrested at a meeting where they were discussing the establishment of a co-op bakery.

Altogether that month the Palmer Raids

scooped up 10,000 people in 70 cities, with members of the IWW, the Amalgamated Clothing Workers, and the International Ladies Garment Workers unions coming in for particular attention.

Meanwhile, the steel strike went on, despite management's *Open Shop Review* journal ceaselessly charging that the strike was entirely "an effort of anarchists…to destroy the government." Senator Miles Poindexter, from the state of Washington, echoed this claim, warning that, unless the federal government did something to suppress the strike, "There is a real danger that the government will fall."

Finally, on January 8th, the great steel strike ended. Beaten, jailed, shot, and starving, the steelworkers were finally broken and they straggled back to work. In the end, 350,000 steelworkers, fighting for the right to collectively bargain with their bosses, were no match for the united opposition of giant corporations, the police and military powers of the state, the judiciary, and the unanimous voice of the mass media – all of whom proclaimed that the steelworkers' hope for a say in their working conditions was a mortal threat to the Republic. The hope of unionizing the American steel industry – and, in fact, organizing the unskilled immigrant workers in all the mass production industries that increasingly dominated American economic life – was defeated. In mill after mill, steelworkers were forced to personally appear before mill managers and apologize for going out on strike, while pledging never to do so again. And, as Robert K. Murray noted, “one fact was universally agreed on – the words ‘revolution’ and ‘bolshevism’ had killed all chance of the strikers’ success.”

Indeed, noted Murray, by the end of 1919, everywhere in America, “all strikes, regardless of their nature, had come to be considered ‘crimes against society,’ ‘conspiracies against the government,’ and ‘plots to establish communism.’” A long night of repression fell across the land, not only upon the American labor movement, but also upon America itself.

The Long Struggle

The year 1919 had been a year of hope and fear – a year of both great hopes for millions around the world, and great fear for millions of others. The coming decade of the Twenties would usher in an era of Republican ascendancy in America and severe repression of the labor movement. The high hopes of millions for a better post-war world in the immediate aftermath of the Great War were crushed. The American labor movement declined drastically over the course of the 1920s, with union membership falling by over two million by the end of that decade.

In the subsequent presidential election of 1920, Republican candidate Warren G. Harding swept to victory with the largest majority to that date in a presidential election. His vice presidential running mate (who himself would soon become president) was Calvin Coolidge, the man who had gained national acclaim by crushing the Boston police strike.

It would not be until the 1930s that Democrat Franklin D. Roosevelt, whose home had been damaged in the anarchist bomb wave of 1919, would offer America a "New Deal" that promised to bring about the new era for which so many workers hoped for in 1919.

But the hope of the New Deal was also, in

its turn, accompanied by the fear of creeping socialism, of incipient communism, which the New Deal represented to many appalled American conservatives. This, however, had been the case long before the Thirties and, indeed, long before 1919.

In 1848, as a previous continent-wide wave of insurrections wracked Europe, Karl Marx and Frederick Engels published *The Communist Manifesto*. That famous pamphlet began with the statement that, "A specter is haunting Europe – the specter of Communism."

The specter of communism, of socialism, has haunted America almost as long, in fact, ever since the 1870s. The 15th Amendment, giving African-American men the right to vote, became law in 1870. The newly enfranchised black voters in the South then began voting for things like public schools, public hospitals, and other types of public improvements that were almost completely absent in the South at that time. These would be paid for by property taxes. These taxes were principally borne by whites, as they owned most of the property in the post-war South. Southern whites almost immediately began charging that such wealth redistribution – or any other similar public improvements – was "socialism."

They had a convenient socialist specter to point to. In 1871, in the wake of the Franco-Prussian War, the Paris Commune ruled Paris for a brief period of socialist euphoria before the

French army brutally suppressed it. But the fear of such a socialist specter lived on to haunt the imaginations of both Europeans and Americans.

When the Great Uprising of 1877 – a nation-wide rebellion against the greed and capitalist rapacity of the Gilded Age – tore at American society in the biggest insurrection in United States history (other than the Civil War itself), political conservatives and the mass media hysterically portrayed it as socialism – the "Paris Commune" – come to America.

And, as we have seen, this same fear, now going under the name of "Bolshevism," manifested itself again in 1919. In his study of the 1919 Red Scare, Robert K. Murray quoted a British journalist resident in America that year. "No one who was in America as I chanced to be, in the autumn of 1919," the journalist observed, "will forget the feverish condition of the public mind at that time. It was hag-ridden by the spectre of Bolshevism."

Indeed, by that time any challenge to the *status quo* had come to be tarred with the label of "Bolshevism," as a poem that appeared in the July, 1919, issue of one popular magazine noted:

"You believe in votes for women?
The Bolsheviki do.
And shorter hours? And land reforms?
They're Bolshevistic, too.
'The Recall' and other things like that,
Are dangerous to seek.

Don't tell me you believe'em or
I'll call you Bolshevik!
Bolshevik! Veek! Veek!
A reformer is a freak!
But here's a name to stop him
For it's like a lightning streak.

And so, also, did political conservatives label the New Deal of the 1930s as yet a newer manifestation of the socialist specter. And – for almost a hundred years – American political conservatives have fought ever since against the "socialist" reforms of the New Deal. Any similar new legislation – such as, for instance, health care reform ("socialized medicine") – that attempts to benefit the public at large faces the charge of being yet another manifestation of red "socialism" threatening the purity of the American economy and society.

The year of hope and fear that was 1919 is not, therefore, ancient history. It was, instead, one more battle, a major battle, an illustrative battle, in the same long and still continuing struggle in America between the hope by many of a better world for all – and the fear by others that this hope might triumph.

About the Author

Eric Leif Davin, Ph.D., is the author of *The Great Strike of 1877; Crucible of Freedom: Workers' Democracy in the Industrial Heartland, 1914-1960; Radicals in Power: The New Left Experience in Office*; and, with Staughton Lynd, *Picket Line and Ballot Box: The Forgotten Legacy of the Labor Party Movement, 1932-1936*. He is also the author of *The Paterson Strike Pageant: An IWW Novel of Bohemia and Insurgent Labor*.

His essay, "The Very Last Hurrah: The Defeat of the Labor Party Idea, 1934-1936," appeared in *"We Are All Leaders: The Alternative Unionism of the Early 1930s,"* (University of Illinois Press, 1996), edited by Staughton Lynd. It won the Eugene V. Debs Foundation's prize as the best essay of that year reflecting the enduring spirit of Eugene V. Debs.

www.ingramcontent.com/pod-product-compliance
Ingram Content Group UK Ltd.
Pitfield, Milton Keynes, MK11 3LW, UK
UKHW040028200726
13854UKWH00001B/410